SOMETIME LIGHT FINDS US

PAMBANA MASAME

Copy right @2022 Pambana Masame
P O Bx 601 AAH Masa, Gaborone
Tel: 267 73612905
pmasame@gmail.com
www.pambanamasame.co.bw

Published by
Corporate Intervention (Pty) Ltd
corporateintervention@gmail.com
+276 71612905

Edited and Proof read
Chris Voysey
Chris Voysey Communications
chris@chrisvoysey.com

First Edition
ISBN: 978-99968-65-79-4

DEDICATIONS

This book is dedicated to my wife, two daughters and a son, who I hope will enjoy a world in which leadership is taken more seriously and carried out more selflessly and purposefully.

Table of Contents

CHAPTER ONE

Baruti Tau was the most popular drunkard in Gaborone and beyond. His popularity rested on his ability to make everybody laugh when he was heavily drunk, which was always a negligent act.

As the first child of his Father, Baruti always had it in mind to break the barrier of poverty and austerity, which was a significant feature of his father's lifestyle when he was alive.

His Father, Mooketsi Tau, was one of the early religious leaders of Gaborone; he was one of the seven men who Gaborone people criticized for accepting the strange belief a group of white men (and a few black people) had brought from the Village of Molepolole - a belief in one son of God called Jesus. The Gaborone people and their traditional ruler met this doctrine with disbelief. The traditional ruler had warned everybody not to accept such doctrine, which was meant to steal them away from the deities of their ancestors, who were their actual owners.

Seven men in Gaborone allowed the missionaries into their homes and were convinced by their doctrines, and the men, together with their families, were converted. Mooketsi Tau, the father of Baruti

Mooketsi, was one of them, and he was the most devoted and committed person to the strange religion that had come to Gaborone. The people of Gaborone criticized Mookesti more than the other six men who accepted the Christian religion because of his commitment and passion for it. He was the first person to be ordained a Pastor in Gaborone after assuring the missionaries that he was ready to engage fully in the work of Christ.

Everybody in Gaborone thought that Mooketsi did that because he was jobless and lived in abject poverty with his family before the missionaries came.

'We all know Mooketsi is a wretched man who finds it difficult to swallow food with meat, so why wouldn't he accept what a white man has brought, knowing full well that the white men will not watch over him and will let his family die in penury,' someone would say.

'An idle hand is indeed a vacant workshop; if Mooketsi has a farmland to cultivate, he would not have accepted a miserable offer from the foreigners,' another person would respond.

Baruti was always sad whenever he remembered these things about his father, Mooketsi, and he always soliloquized, 'I wish I did not have that man as a father. A man who was supposed to be a man for his family and hometown, he shamelessly acted like a bastard of Gaborone by being a traitor and a coward. I regret having him as a father. But I'm happy I'm not like him. My masculinity remains sacrosanct for my family and my people any time, any day'.

What Baruti hated most was cowardice and timidity, which led to unpalatable life compromises. Whenever his first son Tumelo Tau tried to behave like a woman, he always preached it like a sermon to him that 'the greatest calamity that could ever befall a man in life is to lose his manly position and occupy the position meant for women.'

Tumelo, as he was fondly called by many, liked his father's chivalry and courage. He liked his strength and his manly acts. However, Tumelo never ceased to wonder why his father, who possessed all these invaluable qualities, was still a heavy drinker of alcohol.

He was not the only one who kept wondering why his father was a drunkard. friends, families, neighbors, and villagers wondered, too, and Tumelo's awareness that his father's drunkenness was the topic of discussion for market women, street hawkers, and spinsters (whom he thought should be thinking of going to their husband's houses instead of making themselves a bunch of jobless gossips), always made him sad.

Tumelo was twenty-one, a young boy who captivated every girl during his secondary school days. He got the attention of many, including Teachers and people who came for Teaching-Practice. His personal achievements as a student earned him the popularity he had as a student of Hill Crest Secondary School, commonly called Hill. He won many awards both as a junior student and as a senior student when he was in form 3. He was a genius in Art Subjects, the best in English Language, Literature-in-English, and History, which was why his English Language Teacher, Mrs Tale advised him to study Law at the university. Still, he had told Mrs Tale that he had never dreamed of becoming a Lawyer.

Everything about Tumelo was antithetical to his secondary school days. The Tumelo everybody knew to be garrulous would then just decide to be laconic sometimes. His classmates knew him to be outspoken, but sometimes he would behave like an introvert. He was a cheerful type, but sometimes he appeared gloomy to his classmates, and these contradictory behaviours made his classmates confused about him. Tumelo found a friend in his mother, Lesedi Tau, and he was always determined to make his mother happy and proud to have him as a son. Indeed Lesedi was always happy about everything concerning Tumelo. She had danced several times without drums to celebrate Tumelo's various academic breakthroughs when he was in Hillcrest.

Numerous awards were won by Tumelo, some for his outstanding success in debates, some for a brilliant performance in quiz competitions. He was also the goalkeeper of the Hill Football Team, and his proficiency in goalkeeping enhanced his popularity beyond Hill. Whenever Tumelo brought an award or plaque home, his mother would cuddle it like a bosom friend and sing praise songs to God, supporting it with dancing.

Lesedi was a beautiful lady when Baruti first married her. She was slim, tall, and fair-complexioned, and she had an opening between two of her teeth which her friends Onalenna and Gorata referred to as maize teeth. Lesedi met Baruti when she was just eighteen. For the handsome appearance of Baruti, his eloquence, and his sense of humour, Lesedi fell in love with him and admired him more than she had ever admired any man. When Baruti expressed his admiration towards her, she agreed immediately to marry Baruti Tau, the son of Mooketsi Tau – a marriage that had led to much joy with the birth of her three children: Tumelo, Fenyang, and Maureen, her only daughter.

Unfortunately, this marriage that served as a channel to the birth of her three admirable children also served as time went on to be the entrance to a place of endless sorrow and perpetual dejection, which was connected to the drunkenness of her husband Baruti, whom everybody in Gaborone referred to as 'Baruti the street bachelor'.

CHAPTER TWO

Fenyang, the younger brother of Tumelo, was still washing the plates they ate with when he saw three people, a man and two women, heading towards their house. It was about 9 pm, already late, and passersby were few on the street. Fenyang focused on the plates he was washing because he did not like most elderly people in Gaborone. They would constantly castigate you if you didn't greet them; whenever you did, they would say you did not prostrate, and whenever you prostrated, they would say you did not prostrate well enough, but meanwhile you had done it like someone planting maize - unlike Serowe, where the Tau's nuclear family had lived before they came back to Ayedaade their hometown, where people don't attach much value to prostrating for elderly people.

It is not part of their culture in that part of Botswana, and even some Gaborone people over there no longer demanded it from younger ones since they were used to greetings and salutations among people without prostrating or kneeling. Although some Gaborone elders still demanded it in Serowe, many juveniles in Serowe, (like Fenyang and his friends), hated this practice passionately.

Maureen, who had just come out of the kitchen, was already on her knees greeting the three elderly visitors whose reasons for visitation were not yet known. Fenyang reluctantly prostrated and greeted them too, and after the visitors had pronounced some Blessings on them, the man among them asked,

"Where is your Mother Lesedi, is she at home?"

"Yes, sir, she is at home," Maureen replied.

"Tell her we want to see her," one of the women said.

Maureen rushed into the house as if she knew the reason why they were looking for her mother, although she didn't. She met her mother in the living room, already coming outside. She had overheard the conversations and knew there were visitors, but the reason for visitation was also unknown to her.

"Good evening, Lesedi", the women greeted her almost simultaneously.

"Good evening Papa. Good evening, my dear people of Gaborone!!" Lesedi replied.

"Good evening, my daughter," said the elderly man. "Unfortunately, we come to inform you that your husband Baruti is heavily drunk again, and this time around, the effect of the drinks he consumed is so strong on him that he has been going to people's houses, demonstrating what I won't call drunkenness but outright madness!"the man said. And just as if Fenyang wasn't concerned about the news, he was concerned with how people should talk. He immediately asked himself; 'is this how an elderly Man should present matters?'

"More reasons why I dislike most elderly people," he grumbled.

"Lesedi," one of the women tapped Lesedi's shoulder, "None of us came here to make you sad; we only came to call you so that you can go and bring Baruti home. He's really embarrassing himself out there."

"It was a hilarious scenario," the other woman narrated. "Baruti, your husband went to people's houses telling them he wants to drink water, and when the women in those houses gave him water, he told them the water he wanted to drink is the water in their breasts. The first woman he said that to moved closer to him and gave him a dirty slap on his face. He repeated the same statement for another woman, and that one poured the water she first offered him on his head."

The first woman became furious and interrupted her, "Will you stop all this? Do you want to start mocking this woman or what?"

Fenyang was now at the apex of fury. He wished to devour the second woman who was so sarcastic in her narration if there had been cultural restrictions. He hated the woman instantly.

"But the truth must be spoken," the woman replied as if she was really prepared for what was beginning to appear as mockery rather than concern for the Tau Family.

"Keep the dirty, stinky truth to yourself," Fenyang blotted out, and when his mother looked at him with an angry face, he kept quiet. Still, Maureen was happy with Fenyang's action because she also felt like insulting the woman for her infuriating sarcasm.

"I thank you all for the dishonour and the disregard. For turning everything upside down in my presence and almost creating a topsy-turvy scene." The elderly man said sarcastically.

"We are sorry, Papa," the two women, Lesedi and Maureen, said almost simultaneously, but the angry Fenyang did not trsut himself to talk.

It was at this time that Tumelo returned from Dineo's house. Dineo was his closest friend, the only friend he had made in Gaborone since he left Serowe. Although there were many youths like him to make friends with, they were people he did not know, and one has to be careful in making friends with people in an environment that is still new.

The elderly man repeated the matter to Tumelo, and he was immediately lugubrious.

"You have to go and bring your father back home. Otherwise, he'll sleep outside tonight,"

Lesedi comfortably told Tumelo.

Was the comfort really there? Maybe not. comfort would seem to be an illusion of the mind to Lesedi, a woman whose predicament had led her to conclude that comfort is something that merely appears to be there but is not really there.

It was the first time Lesedi said something about the matter that night, but Fenyang and Maureen were not surprised. Whenever issues relating to their father's drunkenness arose, their mother would not say anything until she saw her first son Tumelo.

"Where is he now?" Tumelo asked the man.

"He's at Kealaboga's Shop; he slept beside the Kerosene tank at the front of her shop, that was where we last saw him, and I believe he's still there," the man said.

"Fenyang, let us go." Tumelo and Fenyang left with the man and the two women.

Maureen wanted to follow them, but Tumelo stopped her. She loved her father but it was not right for a young woman to go. Lesedi and Maureen were still standing at the front of their house when Tumelo and Fenyang carried their father back home. Tumelo carried him on his back while Fenyang supported him with his hand so that neither Tumelo nor their father would fall to the ground, but unfortunately, they fell twice before they got home.

As the two Boys struggled to take him in, Baruti started singing the songs he had been singing since he got drunk that day. That was around 2 pm when he started asking women to give him breasts to suck.

"But mummy, Dad always said Stika Sola of Dukwi is his favourite musician; why is he now singing the song of Sangweni of Durban tonight?" Maureen asked her mother.

"Will you shut your mouth if you don't have something reasonable to say?" snapped Maureen. For God's sake, when will this girl grow up and start thinking? "At fifteen, you don't feel the shame of having a father who continuously drinks himself to madness. All you know is eat every food in the house and say rubbish whenever you want to say something." It seemed Lesedi was really willing to transfer aggression on Maureen that night.

"Sorry, Mother," Maureen said gently.

Tumelo and Fenyang carried their father to the bedroom, and after that, nobody said anything to anybody again that night. The house was as silent as a graveyard except for some times when Baruti made some nonsensical utterances from his sleep. The children silently went to bed, but their mother, Lesedi, sat up all night and wept.

CHAPTER THREE

People are just as happy as they make up their minds to be. The unpleasant occurrences that continuously happen in the family of Baruti Tau could not steal the Joy and the Happiness of Tumelo, the first son in the nuclear family. He was always ready to face whatever came his way and determined not just to be happy but joyful because situations and circumstances should not determine people's joy in life.

Tumelo would wake up early to observe what he called quiet time. In the quiet time, he offered prayers of thanksgiving, the forgiveness of sins, provision of material things, and divine blessings on his parents' occupations; then, the Lord's Prayer would be the conclusive part of the prayer. Such is the order of Prayers and the traditional way of praying learnt by children both in the orthodox and the protestant churches.

Tumelo was still observing his quiet time when he noticed someone had sat on one of the big chairs in the living room; he immediately said the Lord's Prayer and opened his eyes to see who it was. It was his father; he sat right beside Tumelo, with his round face, which was always unreadable. He kept his face like that whenever he was at home, and nobody could quickly tell when he was happy or sad because his face was always like that.

Tumelo greeted him, and he responded with that masculine voice which made Tumelo and Fenyang believe that he preferred masculinity to feminity and manliness to being Effeminate.

"Tell your mother I want to see her now!" he roared.

"It seems she's still in bed. Should I wait for her to come out of her room, or I should knock at her door?" Tumelo stammered.

"You are a bastard, and I've always known that! How dare you consider the convenience of a woman at the expense of my own wish, even in my own house?"

"I'm sorry, sir." Tumelo ran to his mother's room and knocked on the door with all his strength as if that would appease his angry father, but when the door was opened, he smiled at his mother as if nothing had happened; Lesedi smiled too and said; "How was your night dear?"

"It was fine; sorry for not saying good morning to you first; it's becoming habitual for me always to smile whenever I look at your face."

"I'm not offended, son; your smile is more precious to me than your greetings."

"Dad says he wants to see you."

"Where is he?"

"He's in the living room."

Lesedi thought Baruti was speaking with somebody on the phone, but she was surprised to see him sitting without a phone in his hand or at the centre of the table in the living room. He was always on the alert; whenever his phone rang, he picked it up very fast before anyone offered to help him get the phone from the table, and if his wife were around at such times, he would rush out like someone who wanted to throw up, so that she wouldn't hear his conversations with his caller because most times, his callers were his various concubines.

"Good morning," Lesedi bent her knees downwards, unlike when they first got married when she would wake early in the morning and say with an affectionate and adoring smile, 'Good morning my King, my Head, the giver of my Bride price'. That was then when Baruti was still in his right mind, their home was still in order, and everything was not as frantic as it had become. Unlike now that his drunkenness had exceeded climax. This time around, he had reached the apogee of his drinking career (after all, he handled drinking as one would handle a career).

Lesedi reflected on these, and Baruti spoke after grumbling for no reason or a reason best known to him.

"I want to tell you that I shall be leaving Gaborone today. Take care of the children," Baruti said authoritatively.

"Baruti! How can you just wake up one morning and announce your departure from your hometown to your family like that?" Lesedi asked rather furiously.

"It is my life, not yours, I can decide to do anything with my life, and it is none of your business."

"Good morning Dad; I think courtesy and some sense of responsibility demand that you speak kindly to your wife and not shout at her like a slave." Maureen cut in.

Baruti smiled. "Come, my daughter, I did not shout at her; I only explained things to her."

"You should have done that in a more civilized manner," Maureen said as she sat on his lap.

"Alright, my darling, I will correct that next time," he said.

Baruti opened his briefcase and brought out oodles of money tied with rubber bands into bundles; he counted and shared the money, handing them over to Lesedi as he specified the reason for each amount he gave her. She collected it reluctantly and sat down with her right palm under her chin, still looking at Baruti with a very angry face. He sent for Tumelo and Fenyang, and when they came, he gave them their pocket money as if he was tipping a salesperson or a Hotel receptionist. He also gave them the money to register for the forthcoming exams they were preparing for.

'Now, I will read as if my life depends on reading, and I can't afford to fail again. This is my third time sitting for O-level exams, and I must make it this time around. My secondary schoolmates are all in college already. I will also ensure I blast the O- Levels so help me, God.' Tumelo thought.

Baruti had gone to the bathroom to take his bath, and Lesedi had reluctantly gone to the kitchen to prepare breakfast. Fenyang was still getting set foro school (he was still in high school) but he was also a prospective candidate for the University entrance exam Tumelo was anticipating. He would participate, and if he were taken, he would have finished high school before the resumption of the first-year students. Maureen was already set for school. She was fifteen years old and in the first year of senior secondary school.

Since she joined Hillcrest High School, the best Private school in Gaborone, she had been settled on as the prettiest girl in the school. Aside from that, she was brilliant, and she came out first in all the subjects she took in her first session as a student of Hillcrest Hight School, which earned her a lot of respect from her fellow students.

Fenyang was also the best in his class. They called him Doctor because he was a brilliant student and a genius in medical science subjects like Biology and Chemistry, and he was very popular.

The Principal of Hillcrest High School , Mr Thomas Khumalo, always boasted about Fenyang and Maureen; he once said on the Assembly Ground; 'I am proud of the Diritos; they are indeed the best students in this school so far. They joined not quite long, and they have obviously become indomitable to their classmates and even their seniors. They are also hardworking; please, I implore you to emulate their good conduct'.

Baruti left that morning in his Mazda 626 Saloon Car. He always dressed corporate like a Bank Manager, and people hardly believed he was a mere driver. He was a driver in the regional branch of Acess Bank, a fast-growing commercial bank in the country. He got the job when he was in Serowe with his family, and after his eight years in service, he requested a transfer to Gaborone, and he was transferred to the new branch of the Bank that was established in Gaborone, his hometown.

CHAPTER FOUR

Tumelo started finding it easy to move freely in the streets of Gaborone after the sudden journey his father had embarked on, unlike when the news of his father's intoxication and insensible acts had spread like a contagious disease in Gaborone, and he would be ashamed of himself as if he was the one who got drunk.

At such times, he found it difficult to go out and even to accompany his mother to the market as he always did. All for his father's shame on the family by his perpetual drunkenness. Nobody was home, and his mother had gone to the Gaborone market to hawk cold drinks and sachet water. That was the business she fell back on after food selling was unsuccessful.

Fenyang and Maureen had gone to school, and Tumelo was the only one at home. He decided to visit Dineo. When Dineo saw Tumelo approaching the almond tree at the front of their house, he smiled and reached for the sachet of cream biscuits beside the big Oxford Advanced Learners Dictionary on the table in front of him. While opening the sachet, he took out three and ate them in quick succession.

"Is that to prevent me from eating your biscuit?" Tumelo asked, noticing and pretending to be serious.

"Yes I don't want you to eat my biscuits with me; I have another food for you," Dineo replied, still crushing the biscuits in his mouth.

"Which food is that?" Tumelo asked.

"Fried Lizard and urine," Dineo replied.

Tumelo looked around to find something he could use on Putsu, a heavy object he could hit him with. Dineo ran into the kitchen and came out again after screaming apologies behind closed doors. They both laughed and exchanged warm handshakes.

"Dineo, you read a lot; you'll even read a dictionary the way you read other books."

"Not so, my friend; I saw some grammar in a magazine I read yesterday and want to check their meanings."

Dineo was the only son of his parents. He was tall, slim and eloquent. He was a high flyer and well-known by almost all his friends and families as dogged and tenacious. He tried his best regarding morality and had much disinclination for every form of an immoral act. He was twenty-one, the same age as Tumelo, but Tumelo was two months older than him. They finished their secondary school education the same year but not in the same school. Tumelo finished in Swaneng English at Serowe, while Dineo finished in Botlhale High School Gaborone.

His uniqueness among the Gaborone youths prompted Tumelo to make friends with Dineo. Dineo was a gentle type, kind and easygoing. Girls in Gaborone called him SU, Moengele, Holy-holy, Saint-Dineo and the likes, all because Dineo would not reciprocate the attention they gave him and their numerous advances towards him.

Girls in Gaborone thought Dineo was just being too serious with life and too religious; some even saw it as pride. But far from it, Dineo was a humble guy, and he just did not have a flare for women; maybe it's true that he was too severe with life because Dineo believed as a young man, there were better things to do with one's time and one's life than womanizing. Even as a secondary school leaver, he was yet to have his first girlfriend, and to the surprise and sometimes discomfort of some people who knew him, he was still a virgin.

"When is your dad coming back?" Dineo asked.

"Coming from where?"

"From where he travelled to, of course."

"How did you know he travelled?" Tumelo asked.

"Our gossips in Gaborone have not retired."

Dineo disliked many people in Gaborone, usually for some lifestyles of theirs, which he considered immoral. He disliked the gossips, the back-biters, the smokers, and the promiscuous men and women in Gaborone. He even had a more severe dislike for young boys and girls in Gaborone who commit what he called fornication in the name of dating. He hated drunkards, too, but he never showed it whenever Tumelo was around.

"He didn't tell us when he would return; he only told us he'd spend about three weeks there," Tumelo explained.

"Alright, just make sure you always pray for him."

Dineo always talked about prayers and the word of God, and things like that were usually boring to Tumelo. He always wished Dineo could talk about something else, but he would not.

"Are you a member of the Scripture Union?" Tumelo asked.

"No, why do you ask?"

"People call you SU, and that's an abbreviation for the religious organization called Scripture Union."

Dineo smiled in a way that showed his upper teeth.

"That is Gaborone people for you! They exaggerate your actions for you, and if they think you are too numinous and Godly, they will start calling you SU. Meanwhile, have you registered?"

"Registered for Scripture Union?" Tumelo raised an eyebrow.

"No! I'm done talking about that, Bro. I mean your Exam." Dineo responded in a more amplified voice.

"I did that yesterday."

"Oh! Great."

"Yeah."

"I wanted to go to the mission house, and Pastor Katlego sent someone to me to say he wanted to see me."

"Then I'll hate to take my leave," Tumelo said.

"You can't take your leave," Dineo said as his voice rose gradually. You'll accompany me to the mission house.

"Well, okay, if that is what you want - I'll accompany you."

"Thanks, Bro."

At exactly 3'O clock, Dineo and Tumelo were already outside the walled compound of The Light of God Church. It was a massive compound with a huge and beautiful gate that anyone would admire at first sight. Every gigantic tower in the church premises that Tumelo could see from outside made him wonder whether Dineo had really brought him to a church or not. How a church building could be that awesome was a question that preoccupied Tumelo.

When the gate was opened, he saw clearly the things that he was merely having a glimpse of when they were still outside the compound. They headed straight to the Pastor's quarters, entered the living room and met Pastor Katlego, who was busy studying the Bible.

"Good afternoon Pastor," Dineo said as he bent his head downwards.

Total prostrating was not needed as far as Pastor Katlego was concerned.

"Oh! Good afternoon, my wonderful Bro Dineo; how are you?"

"I'm fine, Pastor." Dineo smiled in a way that showed his dimples.

Pastor Kat, as he's fondly called, was a kind man, though possessed of a narrow mind. He loved his church and understood his members well, but other religions he could not love or tolerate, and he did not attempt to try. Possessed of a warm and generous nature, he nonetheless found it difficult to extend this nature towards his neighbouring Muslims and Roman Catholics. In the opinion of some critics of Pastor Kat, this had led to the church unwittingly becoming a community turned wholly inwards on itself.

"You are either with us or against us, join us and be saved, oppose us and be doomed," Pastor Kat was fond of saying.

Like other Pastors of his kind in other places, Pastor Kat had never asked himself why it should be him who held the monopoly of divine revelation to the total exclusion of the rest of the human race. He believed he held the truth, and it would have seemed to him the worst form of heresy had he admitted that other religions also might possibly have some access to fundamental truths.

He was a physically small man, possessed of boundless energy, his eyes were a piercing blue, and they shone out with a sparkling freshness from his lined sun-tanned face. He welcomed Tumelo and told him to sit.

"Pastor, you sent for me." Dineo spoke out immediately, remembering that Tumelo had told him they should not stay long.

"Yes, Brother Dineo. Next week Tuesday is Saint Valentine's Day. As the church's Youth Coordinator, I want you to organize an exceptional service for that day. Let it start by 4 PM and end by 9 PM, just five hours. You can incorporate prayers, a joint study of the word of God, a Bible quiz, and other spiritual activities that will bring honour to the lord's name. Do you know how sinners and unrighteous people use days like this to commit all sorts of immoralities? I don't want our youths to be part of such, let us use this program to keep them busy, and they won't be tempted to join the multitude to do evil."

"Yes sir," Dineo was repeatedly saying and nodding in agreement to everything Pastor Kat was saying.

"Plan the program and give me the report in church on Sunday; we shall compel our youths and teenagers to attend. We are special people; why should we have anything to do with sinners?"

Tumelo, who had started noticing the parochiality of Pastor Kat, became tired of his interminable discussion with Dineo.

"I will plan the program and get back to you on Sunday," Dineo quickly cut in.

"Good. How is your Mom?" Pastor Kat asked.

"She's fine, sir," Dineo answered.

"Bro Dineo, go to the kitchen and get cold soft drinks from the refrigerator for your friend and yourself," Pastor Kat said.

"No….no, sir. I'm okay, sir, thanks," Tumelo stammered.

Dineo was not pleased with Tumelo's refusal of the offer. He wanted a drink; in fact, that was one of the things he liked about mission house. There would always be something to eat or drink. Even when Pastor Kat was praying for them, his mind was still on the drink Tumelo had made him lose that day. He could not go to the kitchen to get the drinks since his friend, more of a visitor than he, had rejected the offer. He just managed not to deeply regret that he had brought Tumelo with him to the mission house at all.

CHAPTER FIVE

Tumelo raised himself a couple of inches higher behind the leather-topped desk in the living room and opened one of the oodles of books he had brought out from his room that morning. Ever since he successfully registered for his University entrance exam and had known the date of his Exam, he used almost twenty-four hours a day for reading. He always told himself that he must come out with flying colours.

There was a knock on the door and, on opening, a tall, slim old woman entered, followed closely by a chubby, unattractive young lady. It was Baruti's Mother and his youngest sister. Tumelo seemed not to be surprised to see them, and he knew Grandma could come anytime either to make trouble with his mother Lesedi or to foretell the trouble she could make with her in the nearest future. Whichever one it was, Tumelo was sure of one thing - his Grandma's visit to their home was always unpleasant.

"Welcome, Granny," Tumelo hugged the old woman.

"How are you, my son Tumelo?" The old woman always referred to all her grandchildren with their full names.

"Welcome, Caro," Tumelo said, expecting what his father's younger sister would say.

"Thank you". The fleshy lady said in her baritone voice which made her sound like a man who smokes marijuana.

"Where is your Mother?" The old woman asked as she sat on the nearest seat to Tumelo.

"She is in the kitchen, but dad is not…"

"I did not ask of your father," the old woman interrupted. "Of course, I know my son cannot be home by this time of the day, I taught him how to be dynamic and hardworking, and he has not departed from it. Every other unpleasant thing about him came into his life through his wrong choice."

Tumelo knew Granny was referring to his mother, but he remained calm. He quickly went to the kitchen to fetch his mother, and when Lesedi saw her mother-in-law, she knew the old woman had come to fall out with her as usual. However, she greeted her and her daughter as custom demands, but the duo responded with utmost disdain.

"Lesedi, sit down; I have come to see you for something important to me and my son Baruti," the old woman started. Lesedi sat down quietly. 'If I offer her something to eat or drink, she would reject it and even insult me, so let me just keep quiet', she mumbled to herself.

"Baruti is my first child," the old woman continued. "He is the first proof of my fertility as a woman, the first reason for my permanent stay in the Tau family till today. Why should I keep silent and watch you ruin his life for me?"

"I beg your pardon, Grandma," Lesedi said hurriedly. "Baruti is as important to me as he is to you; he is my husband, the first man to see my nakedness, and my children's father. So, I cannot ruin his life."

"Good! You said he is your husband; now tell me, what have you done as a wife to stop the drinking attitude that has made him a laughing stock in the whole Gaborone?"

At this point, the old woman started shouting at the top of her voice, and some neighbours heard her voice from their different apartments.

"I did not turn Baruti into a drunkard; why should I be responsible for changing him? Am I God that changes people's lives?" Lesedi spoke with apparent anger.

"When my son first brought you home, I did not like you because I knew you and your mother must have bewitched him through the evil palm wine she was selling then, and that was how you both made my son fall in love with you. Ordinarily, my own son Baruti Tau could not have married the daughter of someone who sells palm wine, and he came from a faith home; his father was a pastor in a vibrant church, and we taught him the way of God. He could not possibly have learnt drunkenness but you seduced him and kept giving him your Mother's God-forsaken palm wine until you turned him to a drunkard right there in your mother's shop."

The old woman had already created a scene and was screaming, sounding like she had been seriously cheated. Of course, she felt cheated, she felt Lesedi and her mother cheated her by destroying her massive investment in her first son. She believed Baruti would have been better than he was and even more successful. She thought her son probably would have become one of the principal officers of the Bank where he worked as a driver had he not met Lesedi and dropped out of secondary school. She would always link her son's misfortune with his decision to drop out of secondary school, leave home for a nearby village where he rented a room and camped with Lesedi almost weekly.

"You made my son - a Pastor's child - to keep committing sexual immorality, or was it not pre-marital sex that led to the pregnancy of your first child? His father conducted many wedding programs for other people's children, but you and your witch of a mother did not allow him to organize a wedding for his own son. You have done enough evil to my family and me; leave my family alone. Leave my son's house and let him marry a woman that can tell him to stop drinking alcohol!" Iya agba shouted even more loudly.

"Mama, you have been telling her to leave this house for long, but it seems she will not leave easily, get another wife for my brother and bring that wife to this house; maybe by then, she will leave." Caro said this and gave a long hiss after looking at her sister-in-law with apparent antipathy.

"Mother, just make sure you don't waste your energy talking to a fool who neither has a pleasant past to draw encouragement from nor a bright future to hope for. Don't talk to someone whose tomorrow has already left yesterday," Tumelo gave a long hiss.

Caro's blood was up, she wanted to descend on Tumelo and devour him, but the old woman cuddled her from behind, begging her to leave Tumelo alone and let them face his mother only.

"My God will deal with you and your shameless daughter who has the guts to come to my husband's house and insult me," Lesedi shouted.

"You must leave my son's house…" The old woman shouted as she went out, holding Caro tightly on her wrist in case she flew off and descended on Tumelo again. She was never afraid of fighting with men. She had fought with many men in Gaborone and had overpowered them. People who did not like Caro had gossiped that the two reasons that had cheated her of a husband to marry were her fatness and her warlike behaviour. She's too fat! Some Gaborone men would say. And too rascally! Others would respond.

"Leave us alone and mind your business!" Lesedi shouted from the corridor.

Grandma and Caro heard that from far away. Caro wished she could go back and continue the fight, but the old woman was done for that day. She did not release Caro's hand till they got home.

CHAPTER SIX

The sluggishness of a Camel is not laziness but gentility. Pride is loss; humility is gain. This was one thing Lesedi Tau always reflected on whenever she felt like confronting her husband on the issue of his drunkenness.

She was never happy with Baruti's lifestyle, especially his drunkenness and promiscuity, which he was known for in Gaborone and the places they had lived before. She loved her husband and had vowed to herself from the outset of their marriage that she would never oppose him in anything he did or chose to do. She vowed never to disrespect or disobey him, and all she was doing was just being faithful to her vows.

The elders in Gaborone called Lesedi the Dove because of her gentility. On several occasions, they had told her that her humility and gentility would make way for her wherever she found herself.

'Some women would have divorced their husbands if they experienced the shame and embarrassment this poor woman had experienced as Baruti's wife,' one elder would say.

'She has excellent endurance and is the most courageous woman I have ever seen,' another elder would say.

The desire to stop Baruti Tau from drinking alcohol always rose up within Tumelo. Still, he felt there was nothing anybody in their house could do about it since they were all victims of the domestic tyranny Baruti consistently demonstrated.

'He is a man nobody in this family can advise,' Tumelo would say to himself.

When Baruti is speaking, no one dares interrupt. Nobody was allowed to object or suggest anything. No one dared ask him questions or oppose his decisions. He was dictatorial and highly inflexible. How then could anybody have told him to stop drinking? The last time Fenyang told him to stop chasing women, he gave him the beating of his life. When they first returned to Gaborone after his transfer, and Tumelo told him to reduce the rate at which he was drinking back in Serowe, he almost beat him to death; if he dared mention such to him again, it might have been the end of Tumelo.

"I'm sure he would kill me," Tumelo would mumble.

"A city is what it is because its citizens are what they are," Fenyang once said to Tumelo as he sat beside him on his bed, while he was thinking about their father's unruly lifestyle.

"So what does that teach us?" Tumelo asked.

"This family is what it is because we, the members, are what we are. This family is under a dictatorial leader; tyranny and autocracy prevail in this family, our father uses his power as a father without regard for anybody's opinion or feelings, and I am sure this has not stopped because his children and our mother are yet to take any action," Fenyang said as he began sounding like an activist ready for a revolutionary protest.

" Fenyang, are you trying to say we should stop Dad from acting as the father in this house?" Tumelo asked.

"That is not what I'm saying, Bro. He should at least allow us to speak our minds on certain issues, listen to our advice sometimes, and start considering our opinions too; we are not slaves; we are his children, for crying out loud."

"Is that all?" Tumelo cut in.

"It's not all, Bro. My friends at school influence their parents' decisions; many of them have successfully stopped their parents from doing things they don't like. For examle, Moremi influences her dad's decisions."

"Who is Moremi?" Tumelo asked.

"Don't you remember Moremi, my friend? That girl from Gweta."

"Oh! That's your girlfriend." Tumelo laughed for the first time that morning.

"No, Bro, I told you she declined when I asked her out. She's got a boyfriend," Fenyang said with a worried look that he had just remembered something he didn't like. Despite all his effort, he could still not get that yellow-skinned beautiful Moremi. "Why can't our father give us the chance to speak our mind?" he continued.

"Even our mother cannot interfere in his affairs, let alone we the children."

Tumelo took a long breath and stretched himself on the bed. "Bro, you're not saying anything. What do you want me to say? Whatever I say now obviously cannot change anything about our father, so it's unnecessary."

"But it can show us the way forward," Fenyang said.

"Forward to where?" Tumelo asked.

"To gain freedom of speech and expression for ourselves," Fenyang said hurriedly.

"I am not interested," Tumelo said as he reached for his cell phone on the other side of the bed, unlocked the phone, opened the music folder and glanced through his playlist, where he saw the latest Zimbabwean Rhumba music from his favourite Artiste; Paul Matavire. He hit the play button and danced to the mind-blowing beat of the single while still in bed. Matavire was known for hit jamz.

Fenyang walked out angrily. He was defiant and had been the only one who dared his father several times. Despite all the brutal beatings he had received from him for being confrontational, he was determined never to give up until their barbaric father changed for good.

CHAPTER SEVEN

Fenyang and Maureen arrived home from school the following day to find their mother in a sad mood; she sat with her right foot over her left foot, and both feet were shaking as she sighed repeatedly.

"Good afternoon mother." The children were unhappy at her lethargy and glaring at her.

"Welcome my children; how was school today? Your father is back, and he was brought home by a group of young men from where he got himself drunk."

"Where is he?" Maureen asked hurriedly.

Fenyang turned towards his room and disappeared from his mother's presence.

"I'm going into the bedroom now; he has not opened his eyes since he was brought home," Lesedi said. Maureen rushed into the bedroom and found her father snoring heavily and noisily on the bed. She removed his pair of shoes and called him gently 'Daddy'. Maureen had called her father that since she was three years old. Unlike Tumelo and Fenyang who called their father 'Papa',

Maureen usually called him Daddy. He did not wake up despite how hard Maureen tried to wake him. The room was filled with unpleasant odours of alcohol, an odour everyone in the family was used to and hated.

Tumelo returned from the house of his friend Dineo, and he stayed outside for some minutes thinking of where else to go because he did not wish to be staying at home when his father was there during the day. This was obviously due to Baruti's cantankerous attitude as he would confront anyone in the house with diverse troubles. He easily found fault in people and was always ready to make issues out of everything his wife and children did. It was not really the case that Baruti only did this to his own family alone; he even did it outside too … although, not that often.

His concubines, Lesedi and her children (who thought they would be getting all the love and affection from him) were often victims of his warlike nature. His concubines, however, were patient with him and tried to keep the relationship happy since their major concern was to keep getting money from him. And indeed, they did get money from him. In his first two years in Gaborone after his transfer, he was already having an affair with nine women and, whenever he received his salary, would visit all of them and give them their share as if they all helped him to work for the money. The only thing he took home to his wife and children at the end of every month was a little money and many complaints and murmurings. He would even tell them there is not much profit in his work, as if he were into trade or any business. What else could be the gain of a salary-earning driver if not his salary?

But with the way Baruti had chosen to live his life, he could hardly enjoy his gain or profit even though they gave it to him every month. In Botswana, adultery and fornication are regarded as stealing people's fortune, and it is usually analyzed to collect the gains or profits of one's labour.

Tumelo was trying to sneak into his room when his father came out of the bedroom where he had laid all day like a dead person awaiting the embalming of his body.

"Welcome, Sir," Tumelo stammered. "How are you?"

"I'm fine."

Tumelo gazed at his father; he noticed that he had become more fleshy and heavy, his chest looked wider than it used to be, and his pot belly was not reducing. However, his light skin was fresh, and Baruti, in his fifties, was still a handsome man.

"Where is my daughter?" Baruti asked of Tumelo. Tumelo could not remember the last time he referred to him and Fengyang as his sons, but he always called Maureen his daughter. He prided himself on it.

"She is with mum in the kitchen," Tumelo said hurriedly.

At this point, they both heard the sound of drums and the voices of what seemed to be a crowd coming from outside. They sang Christian songs and supported these with a hard clapping of hands. Fenyang had looked from the window to see the what was happening, and he saw that it was church people; they were out for evangelism and an awareness of their forthcoming crusade. Everyone in that crowd did whatever they were doing with great passion. A more significant part of the crowd were those singing and clapping, and they were the most passionate.

What made Fenyang laugh in his room was when he saw Thabo, the man with one hand, even clapping more than those with two hands. Thabo was an elderly Man who didn't marry nor had any child of his own; he had lost one of his hands many years before in a car accident, and the hand was lifeless and eventually amputated. Thabo's life had been miserable until he secured a security guard job with this church. He had been persuaded to marry but insisted on remaining single. He claimed he was not rich enough, and his salary was not even enough for him, let alone a wife and children. However, Thabo was a passionate Christian; apart from being a security guard in the church's extensive premises, he had become a member of the church; in fact, he had overlapped his duty by joining the church in several other activities, one of which was this very mass evangelism and crusade jingle he joined them for that evening.

How Thabo made more impact in clapping despite having one hand was what made Fenyang laugh. The man would hit one hand on his upper leg, making a loud sound; when he started feeling much pain in the lap he was beating, he would start beating the second lap; that was how he alternated lap beating from one lap to another. Thabo means joyous at birth, and interestingly, this man retained his joy till adulthood despite his various life calamities. Fenyang laughed till he suddenly started feeling compassionate about Thabo's condition and stopped laughing.

Tumelo remembered that Dineo told him they had mass evangelism in their church that evening and would reach every nook and cranny of Gaborone. 'They must be playing those drums,' he said to himself as he brought the glass of water his father had requested. Baruti took the glass of water and gulped it twice. In the distance, the voices continued to sing, and the drums continued to beat.

CHAPTER EIGHT

Bontle Khumo was a very beautiful young lady who combined beauty with arrogance. In the opinion of some persons, she was so arrogant that she refused to mingle or associate with most of her fellow girls in Gaborone. She was the only daughter of Mr Rufus Khumo, a wealthy and benevolent man in Gaborone.

He was a businessman who had lived in Gaborone for twenty-five years. After he graduated from the University, he joined his elder brother Neo in Gaborone. His first four years in Gaborone were already a success story. It was within those years that he established a bakery. He knew how to bake bread right from his early days in Tutume, his hometown, where he had worked in different bakeries to support himself financially. He lost his father when he was eleven years old, and his widowed mother single-handedly catered for him and his siblings. Mr Rufus' bakery was the best, and many people in the neighbouring towns purchased his bread.

The people of Gaborone loved Mr Rufus for bringing development to the land, and his bakery had brought many visitors from far and near. He had achieved a lot in Gaborone, and to him, Gaborone was like the biblical land of Canaan that flowed with milk and honey. He had come to the town as a fresh graduate, but after twenty-five years, there were many fortunes he could point at; his marriage to his beautiful wife Masego, whom he also gave the name Lesego which means Luck. Rufus believed she had brought a lot of Luck to him.

Then, of course, there was also his pretty daughter Bontle and his five great establishments: RUFUS KHUMO BREAD FACTORY, RUFUS BEST ELECTRONICS, a company where various electronic products were sold, KHUMO MICROFINANCE BANK, a financial institution where he was lending money to people with low-interest rates, TREASURE HOTELS AND SUITES and TREASURE SUPERMARKET, a supermarket that his wife managed. All these establishments were on the soil of Gaborone.

The central preoccupation of Mr Rufus mattered to him: to remain the wealthiest man in Gaborone and its environs, to keep helping the poor and supporting various organizations with his money. He was focused more on his act of philanthropy and his relentless efforts to remain an excellent husband to Masego and a good father to his only child Bontle.

Mr Rufus was a man who would not listen to several rumours people sometimes spread about him. When a staff of RUFUS BEST ELECTRONICS died of cancer, people said Rufus had used him for rituals. Many had insisted that Mr Rufus' wealth was beyond ordinary and that it required occultic means to possess such an astonishing wealth.

Pastor Katlego of the Light of God Church had once described Mr Rufus' wealth as God's blessings which is a reward for his generosity towards the poor and the needy, towards the church of God and towards Gaborone. Bontle liked it whenever her father's wealth was mentioned in any gathering, although she only witnessed such in church and school. She finished her secondary school education when she was seventeen. Although her father wanted her to further her education in Nigeria, she insisted on studying abroad, and Mr Rufus agreed. He always wanted to please his only child with all the luxuries he could lay his hands on. Bontle usually felt on top of the world whenever her father's huge donations and charity were announced in her school. The entire school knew she was the only child of the famous philanthropist.

She had grown into what people saw as an epitome of beauty. It had been two years since she finished secondary school and had excellent results in her O-Level. She was nineteen now, tall, light-skinned and facially attractive, at least to every masculine consciousness. She had a kind of rapid growth that is not unusual for a girl child. Since she was sixteen, she had developed the kind of breasts that captured the eyes of several boys in Gaborone. Boys like Richard the rhymer had walked up to her then and had told her how beautiful she was and the rate at which he had sleepless nights because of her. Bontle had ignored Richard on such occasions. (Richard was not even a star rapper; he had not yet risen to stardom; he was just passionate about it and tried his best by organizing free concerts and parties in Gaborone, where he entertained his few audiences. But Richard was full of hope, and he optimistically told himself that he would be great in rap music one day.)

Although people like Modise, the cultist, had been envying Richard and had tried to convince Gaborone youths that he was more talented than him yet, he could not stop Richard's little fame among the youths maybe because not many youths in Gaborone liked Modise and his clique. For many people, Modise and his friends as either cultist or having a flare for cultism since that was what they seemed to represent in Gaborone.

Most Gaborone youths hated cultism and every form of violent lifestyle. Modise had been arrested and locked in a cell sixteen times in four years for cultist-related activities. For reasons like this, Richard had more fans than Modise. His fame may not have gone beyond Gaborone but, at least his charity had begun from home where he had been giving a free entertaining performance to people for years, and he was widely recognized in Gaborone as a rap sensation.

CHAPTER NINE

Kolanut lasts long only in the mouth of those who know and appreciate its value. Baruti Tau being who he was, lost the kola nut in his mouth because he did not know the value, or maybe he knew the value but decided not to appreciate it.

He was dismissed from his working place after committing what the management of Access Bank called a severe crime. He received his salary on a Tuesday afternoon and left the Bank premises after 4 pm. He went straight to one of the places he usually drank his beer. He had withdrawn about half of the salary he received through the Automated Teller Machine and had left with one of the cars that belonged to the bank. Mr Mompati was the most senior driver in the Gaborone branch of Apex Bank, he knew it was illegal to go home with the bank's official cars, but he deliberately allowed Baruti to do so. He had a preference for Baruti, among other drivers in the bank. He favoured Baruti on specific issues and discriminated against other drivers several times.

Moreover, Mr Mompati did all these because he had a common ground with Baruti. He was also a drunkard, but if drinking were a competition, he would never beat Baruti, maybe because he was a stingy man. Most of the beers he had consumed since he met Baruti had been bought by Baruti. Once or twice, they had sneaked out of the Bank premises together to take chilled beers and fried meat. Moreover, it was an open secret. Some of the junior drivers already knew this, and they constantly gossiped among themselves that Mr Mompati was only a glutton who favoured Baruti because of the free drinks he always got from him.

Baruti did not take Mr Mompati with him that day as he wanted to enjoy his money alone. He finished three crates of beer that day with a lot of fried meat. When the Goat meat finished, he requested Cow meat. Many beer joints in Gaborone sold Cow meat to their customers as an alternative to Goat meat. After patronizing about eight beer shops that day, Baruti staggered into the car and drove almost unconsciously to a place he did not know. He was heavily drunk. It was already dark when he suddenly found himself on a quiet tarred road with no street lights like those of other roads in Gaborone which were illuminated by solar-energy lights.

Totally drunk and increasngly unconscious, Baruti placed his head on the car steering to sleep off the effects of his mis-spent afternoon. A car was speedily approaching, but Baruti was too far gone to notice. The car drove past, then suddenly stopped. The engine was switched off and a gang of robbers jumped out. One of them ran back to check who was in the car parked beside the road, and he saw a man in deep sleep with his mouth wide open and thick saliva dripping from it. The others joined him, and one of them opened the front door and carried him out of the car. He placed him beside the road, and they all rushed into the car and drove off but receievd a surprise - the police were already waiting for them, having been informed of their just concluded robbery.

The police pointed their guns toward the robbers and threatened to waste them if they tried anything funny. They would have confronted the police officers, but they were just five men, and the police were many. So, they surrendered and were all handcuffed and taken to the police station that night. Modise was one of them, and it was when people heard the news the following day that they realized that Modise was not just a cultist, but he had added armed robbery to his heinous lifestyle.

The headquarters of Access Bank was informed on Wednesday morning that one of their cars was used for robbery. The bank was sued, although, after several corroborative evidences to prove the bank's innocence in the robbery, the charge against them was dropped. Baruti and Mr Mompati were immediately fired, and other bank drivers were seriously warned against similar acts.

When it happened, Tumelo was not in Gaborone as he had travelled to Francistown for the exams. When he spoke with his mother on the phone, she told him what had happened to his father. He was crestfallen. The worst has happened, he said to himself. Dineo, who also went to Francistown for the exam, was beside him; they had already done their exam and planned to leave the next day.

"What happened?" Dineo asked.

Tumelo told him everything, and they both fell into silence. The silence was broken by a text message on Dineo's cell phone. It was a message from the examination board. (It was a computer-based test, so the results were usually released early and a text message sent to the phone number of candidates). Dineo was nervous but finally opened the message and discovered that he had come out with flying colours.

"I made it!" Dineo announced.

"Congrats!" Tumelo screamed, and he hugged Diego, forgetting the news from home for that moment.

When they returned to Gaborone the next day, Tumelo did not go home immediately. He knew the news would have spread all over Gaborone, and he was ashamed of looking at people's faces, so he decided to go home at night. People knew him as the first son of Baruti Tau and even referred to him as Baruti Junior, but he always rejected it with silent prayers. He would silently say, "God forbid".

It was not that he hated his father, but if there was anything Tumelo did not want in life, it was becoming a man like his father. He kept assuring and reassuring himself that he would never epitomize his father in any way. He personally vowed that all his life, he would never know even what price alcoholic drink is sold for. He was highly determined to remain a teetotaler forever.

He left Dineo's house in the night and Dineo accompanied him They walked together towards the market gate. Dineo's house was close to one of the Gaborone markets. At the market gate, motorcycle riders parked their motorcycles and waited for commuters that they would take to their various destinations. One of them beckoned to Tumelo, but he ignored him. Motorcycle riders are often snubbed by commuters who are either not ready for a ride or dislike their motorcycles, especially the rough and dirty ones. But Tumelo ignored him simply because he was not happy. Dineo found one motorcyclist when they got to the market gate, and he beckoned to the lanky man and insisted that Tumelo mount the transport.

"I will call you when I see my result," Tumelo said as he jumped on the motorcycle.

He was surprised that he did not meet his father at home. He expected that he would meet him in a sober mood, regretting what had happened. But, Fenyang told him that their father was still drinking. And was still coming home late at night, even in spite of losing his job!

"Is this man cursed? Is there a spell of drunkenness on him?" Tumelo could not believe he had just said that.

"It is either something like that or something more than that, and I just know it cannot be less than that," Fenyang said.

"The person in question is our father, and I think he should be respected," Maureen who was standing by said and quickly moved away from Fenyang. Fenyang's blood was up, he raised his hand to swipe at her, but Tumelo grabbed his hand.

"She is correct; courtesy demands that we respect our father," Tumelo said with a cold voice.

CHAPTER TEN

Shortly after the dismissal of Baruti from work, his close friend Boipelo visited him. Boipelo was a short man with a bald head, so short was he that some people usually told him that he was not different from a dwarf, and for his apparent baldness, some people called him Vulture. Being a gentleman, he never picked offence in whatever anyone said about his stature and look.

"Life has to move on, my friend," he told Baruti that morning. "It is about time you got another job, you have a family to take care of, and your mother is still alive, still interested in eating from your wealth as a reward for her motherly efforts on you".

"But I cannot go out and be begging for a job, I still have my self-worth, and I am still very conscious of it," Baruti said with the usual pride that Boipelo had always known him for.

Indeed Baruti was always conscious of who he thought he was. He esteemed himself very highly and disliked being a victim of tyranny and subjugation, though he himslef was a tyrant - a domestic one.

"Looking for a job does not reduce or take away your self-worth, my friend, and if you cannot look for a job, I will do it for you. Moreover, I already have one for you," Boipelo said.

Baruti was not surprised - he knew Boipelo to be a friend who would always go the extra mile to help him even when he did not ask for it. That morning, he remembered the friendly passion of Boipelo when they were much younger, especially the one he demonstrated during Baruti's father's funeral many years before. Boipelo was everywhere that day, and so busy was he that people who didn't know him as Baruti's friend thought that he too was one of the children of the deceased.

"Tell me about the job," Baruti said, staring at his friend with an unreadable look.

"You know I work with the richest man in this town, Mr Rufus Khumo. You know he owns many business firms, and he employs the people of this town more than outsiders. He will soon start his Table Water business. He just finished building the factory, and he is already employing people. He needs a driver too, and you should be one to apply. I am sure he will employ you when he finds out you are from this town and have been a driver for over a decade. I shall also tell him that you are my childhood friend and a good man". Boipelo said, trying to cover his head with his palms as a way to avoid the heat from the sun that was already rising and sneaking in through the window of the living room where they sat that morning. He would feel the hotness more than Baruti since there were little or no hairs on his head to protect him from the painful hotness of the sun. He covered his forehead first which was where he felt the heat the most; it was here where the baldness started.

"Boipelo, are you trying to reduce me to the level of a one-man company?" Baruti asked with a smile.

"Don't get me wrong - I am only trying to render some help here," Boipelo said, warmly.

"How much is the salary?" Baruti asked.

"I don't know, and you will find out when you apply".

Boipelo had worked with Mr Rufus for seven years, he was the chief security at his Hotel, and he had benefited a lot from the benevolence of the Okoye family.

"I hope you can drive well?" Boipelo asked jokingly.

"The chameleon is not afraid of any colour because it is the master of many colours," Baruti boasted, and they both laughed.

Almost immediately, Lesedi appeared; she greeted Boipelo but ignored her husband. Boipelo started his usual exaggerations of Lesedi's beauty and character, and she smiled shyly.

"Our wife, your husband, told me about your sudden change of behaviours towards him," Boipelo continued. "He told me you only give him food twice a day, don't lend him money whenever he wants to borrow, and don't allow him to touch you whenever he wants to …"

"I have not done anything wrong to your friend," Lesedi interrupted. "I give him food twice daily because that is precisely what the money he drops can provide. If he wants a third meal, he should go to the bars where he spent all his money on beer, or better still, to his concubines on the streets whom he always told had no wife at home, and get some money back. As for the money I refused to lend him, I don't think I can lend any money to him.

I hawk soft drinks and snacks in the market to make money, and I will not waste my hard-earned money like he did when he made his own money. I will instead use them for my children's upkeep. I also cannot allow him to touch me, and he should go and meet his concubines, if that is what he wants."

Lesedi said the last comment with the usual attitude of a woman burning with jealousy, and she knew that that was the one that pained Baruti the most. Still, she was happy that she finally had the opportunity to torment him with what he knew to be his weaknesses.

Baruti was silent as his wife spoke. But he was infuriated by everything she was saying, and he regretted that he could not do what he felt like doing to her. Hwoever, although he was very strict, troublesome, and barbaric, Baruti was not a man who would beat a woman. That was one of the reasons why neighbours have never needed to come to Baruti's house to intervene in any of the troubles he made with his wife. He could make trouble with his wife in several dimensions, but it never involved beating her.

Unlike the family in the next building to them, where a man known as Khosy had converted his wife Tale into a punching bag. Sometimes, he wrestled with her, sometimes they exchanged blows, and on several occasions, they fought by destroying the properties the other person bought. Khosy would break his wife's big pots and cooler, and Tale would break their Television and Radio sets. The apogee of their domestic violence was the day Khosy continuously beat Tale till she fainted, and some people who came to separate them thought she was dead. Tumelo would not stop; he escaped from those holding him and descended on Tale with a heavy blow that woke Tale up again. That was why Khosy was referred to, in the neighbourhood, as the man who beats his wife to death and beats her back to life again.

Baruti never took his rapacity to such a level. He hated Khosy for such a lifestyle, which was why he never paid for Khosy's beer whenever he met him in the beer parlour. That was one of the few things he learned from his late father, Mooketsi. "Beating a woman, especially one's wife is nothing but stupidity; men who do such are not different from animals," his father would always say.

"Lesedi, if you want to roast a snake according to its length, you may end up burning the whole house," Boipelo said.

"I know you to be a woman of noble character, your husband may have offended you in many ways, but if you remain vindictive, you may be doing what would negatively affect the whole family. Please forgive him and forget all his past wrongdoings," Boipelo pleaded.

"He did not offend me, but thank you all the same," Lesedi said, leaving the living room and going straight to the kitchen to prepare breakfast. She did not like seeing Baruti's way of life as an offence. Though unknown to many, it was a lifestyle they both started together in her mother's shop more than two decades before.

CHAPTER ELEVEN

Mr Rufus' Water factory started on a Monday morning, and Baruti resumed with other newly employed workers. Mr Rufus had told him to minimize drunkenness if he would work with him for long, but Baruti had refused to say anything during that conversation; he kept quiet until Mr Rufus changed the topic of discussion. That was the sum total of the interview Baruti had before getting this job.

He wasn't subjected to the rigorous interview others were subjected to, maybe because Mr Rufus felt the work of a driver doesn't need such. But one thing was clear to Baruti, and that was the fact that the business tycoon liked him at first sight. Boipelo had told him that Baruti was the man sacked by Access Bank after the recent robbery and the subsequent apprehension of the robbers. He heard the news since he was one of the many customers of Access Bank, but he didn't know the whole story, and when Boipelo told him Baruti was that driver, he quickly added that his friend was innocent. So defensive was Boipelo that he didn't mention that Baruti was drunk when the robbers snatched the car from him. But Mr Rufus knew, in the newspapers, that the Bank driver was heavily drunk when the robbers took the car from him. However, he showed approval almost immediately after seeing Baruti for the first time and decided to employ him after warning him against drinking alcohol.

In spite of all this positivity, Baruti was not comfortable with his new job. 'Rich men can be annoying and always want to control people's lifestyles, especially their employees. But what can I do? I have to accept whatever happens here. The desire to eat yam causes one to keep one's hand inside palm oil,' Baruti thought. He sighed and started work for that day.

That morning, Tumelo went to Dineo's house to tell him his result had been released. His result was withheld for days for a reason he did not know. Dineo was happy to hear that the result had finally been released, and his friend also had qualified to sit for the entrance examination of the school he chose.

However, Tumelo did not like his score, which was below his expectation.

"Surely you should be happy that you can write the entrance exam and get admission than be overwhelmed by scores?" Dineo said.

Tumelo believed that success is all about the number of grounds covered and the number of figures achieved, but Dineo, on the other hand, had a different ideology; he believed that good success was just about doing what is required for continuity. Not that he was mediocre; in fact, he would always tell Tumelo that in the journey of life, we shouldn't do our best; we should do what is required because sometimes, what success demands may be beyond our best.

Tumelo soon stopped worrying about the exam score and focused on having good grades in the O-Leves that had started about three weeks before. He had two papers left and would soon return to the nearby town where his centre was. His brother Fenyang was writing the O-Levels too, but he had finished his own three days before; science students usually finish before the Arts and Social science students. Their mother had sold her crates of empty bottles to her friend in the Gaborone market, who also sold soft drinks. She also sold her clothes, shoes and jewellery. She gave some of her clothes that she couldn't find anyone to buy to the woman who buys used clothes at cheaper rates.

Maureen had been withdrawn from Hillcrest High School and had enrolled in Gaborone Senior Secondary school because their mother could no longer afford the fees at Hillcrest. In Gaborone Senior Secondary School, education was free because it was a public school, and school authorities were not allowed to collect money from students. However, Fenyang did not leave Hillcrest, he had only one term left, and the management awarded him a scholarship for that term. At Hillcrest, whoever comes first in a term would be awarded a scholarship for the next term. However, payment for the O-Levels was excluded, so Lesedi withdrew Maureen and used all the money she gathered to pay for Fenyang and Tumelo's O-Levels.

Things were getting decidedly worse for the Tau family since their father lost his job at Access Bank. There were several nights of going to bed without food. At first, Baruti gave his wife a little money to prepare food to which she added a little every day before the family could feed twice a day. This seemed to be the first time in Baruti's life when it dawned on him that the number nineteen that refuses to be added to number one will find it tough to become twenty. He started realizing that in life, people need one another and that together, people could achieve more. This prompted

Baruti to foster collaboration with his wife, at least for that period of his life.

Lesedi was preoccupied with nothing but dreams about the future of her children. She would ensure they accomplished what she and their father could not. She had also inherited a small piece of land from her family, which she farmed on, and sometimes she would go to the market to hawk boiled groundnuts. She had stopped selling soft drinks since there was no more capital to continue after she had sold all her crates of empty bottles and supplemented the money she got from it with all the money she had at home and used it to pay for her children's exams. She took care of all their needs and even stopped engaging in things that eat money just to ensure her children were educated.

She left the women's group so she would not be forced to spend money on several clothes and fabrics for outings. It was acceptable for a festival in another village that the women's group had distributed a uniform wrapper to all their members. When the group leader came to collect Baruti's payment, she brought the wrapper out from where it had been lying in her bedroom from the day she collected it and gave it back to the group leader.

"I have come to collect the money," the group leader announced.

"I don't have money, so I'm returning the cloth; I've not cut it yet". Lesedi replied coldly.

"Lesedi, calm down. None of us really have this money, and we only join hands to help one another. You will surely need us one day, maybe you should not some and meet us in the meantime," the woman threatened.

"I don't want to be a member of your group again, and I have never seen any good thing that comes out of your group. Please go,"

Lesedi answered. That was the end of women's group activities for Lesedi and the beginning of her self-expulsion from all social groups.

Tumelo accompanied Dineo to see Pastor Katlego that day. It was a week of celebration for the clergyman. He had just convocated in one of the prestigious Universities in the country a day before, and Dineo went to congratulate him on receiving his Doctorate. "It is a great academic achievement, the apex of certified learnings". Dineo had boasted to Tumelo before they both set out for a visit.

"One has to stop wondering why your church is that big; it would be unfair for someone to abandon all his acquired degrees and become a Pastor and end up not having a big church; God is not wicked". Tumelo said as they walked down to the mission house. "I heard his first son is in England. Is it true?" Tumelo asked.

"Yes, his name is Israel; he also graduated from the same University. His dad bagged all his degrees. Pastor sent him to England for his Masters's degree, and he also pastors the branch of our church over there," Dineo explained.

"Is he a Pastor too?" Tumelo interrupted.

"Yes, his father ordained him in his final year."

"So when Pastor Kat is no more, his son will take over as the general overseer, isn't it?"

"I don't know," Dineo snapped. "I hope you are not about to start criticizing the Man of God again; you know I won't have such a conversation with you."

"I am not criticizing; only asking questions about whatever I don't understand about them. Not everyone will be as dogmatic as you.

Dineo, you can believe that a triangle has four sides, without asking questions, as long as it was said in church and by a religious leader," Tumelo said.

Dineo always admired his friend's critical thinking and inquisitive tendencies, but he usually wished Tumelo would stop bringing it into religious matters. He was so religious that he would even try walking without moving his head if such was required for holiness and purity.

Their visit to Pastor Katlego lasted about an hour; although Dineo wanted to stay longer, he could see the eagerness to leave in Tumelo's eyes and always wanted to please his friend. Tumelo was uncomfortable with everything within the one hour they spent in the mission house. Not even the hospitality of Mummy Pastor enticed him. It was common for the Pastor's wife to show kindness to new faces in church; it was one of the strategies for winning more souls and making them feel the love that characterizes the Christian fold. Although she had never seen Tumelo in their church, she still felt the need to extend the agape love to such a promising young man who could also become a vessel unto honour in the house of God if he joined the fold.

What Tumelo did not like that day was the prolonged sermon of Pastor Kat. Dineo had told the Pastor that his friend was not born again and that he wanted him to be one. That was why whenever Tumelo visited Dineo, he would always persuade him to follow him to the mission house. He knew Pastor Kat would always preach to him.

When they came out of the mission house and headed towards the gate, someone opened it and walked in. Tumelo stopped and stared at this girl he had never seen before until she walked past them. She also stared at Tumelo as she climbed the steps leading to the mission house's living room. And before she vanished into the living room, she looked back to see whether Tumelo was still looking at her. Tumelo was still looking with his mouth wide open, as if he was seeing a girl for the first time in his life. When he realized that saliva had started dropping from his widely opened mouth, he quickly closed his mouth and turned to Dineo.

"Who is that girl?" Tumelo stammered.

"That is the peacock I have told you about," Dineo said with obvious contempt.

"Did you just say peacock?"

"Yes. She is a peacock, so proud and arrogant. I don't like her." Dineo proclaimed.

"What is her name?" Tumelo asked.

"Her name is Bontle, and if you wish to know more, she is the daughter of Mr Rufus Khumo, the richest man in this town. Her father must have sent her to the Pastor, and I hardly see her come to the mission house during the week," Dineo narrated.

"Is this the same Mr Rufus that owns the factory where my dad works?" Tumelo asked.

"Yes, it is."

"And she's a member of your church?"

"Of course she is. Her father is a deacon."

Tumelo smiled in a way that confused Dineo, and he whispered to him, "Be expecting me in your church next Sunday."

CHAPTER TWELVE

Bontle sat quietly in the third row of the chairs at the left wing of the church auditorium. It was the last Sunday of the month, and devoted Christian families like the Okoyes always arrived early to church because the last Sunday of every month was prayer Sunday, while the first Sundays are for thanksgiving. Other families also came early to church that day, and Pastor Katlego was ready to lead the church in fire-brand prayers as he always described it.

Dineo was the first person to see Tumelo among the congregation, he was well dressed, and he looked more handsome than Dineo knew him to be. Dineo was standing before the congregation and interpreting for a young man called Festus, who was summarizing the Sunday school lesson taught that morning. Festus spoke in the Tswana language while Dineo interpreted in English.

Tumelo sat in the back seat after politely refusing to sit where one of the ushers initially asked him to sit. He winked at Dineo, but Dineo ignored him for the moment.

"He's too serious," Tumelo mumbled as he started looking around to find Bontle. Dineo noticed his head turning in every direction, and he understood what his friend was up to.

The Sunday school summary section was followed by a prayer section from one of the church deacons, and the prayer section was succeeded by the praise and worship from the choir. Those with testimonies walked up majestically to gladly share them with the church. The elders listened in great delight, the youths with less enthusiasm, the instrumentalists uninterested.

They soon sang the hymn, a section that now captured the interest of the instrumentalists, and after the hymn section, Pastor Kat walked enthusiastically to the podium. He walked behind one of the protocol team members, who carried his Bible and Diary to the podium for him.

Tumelo frowned at this. "It's just pride and nothing less than pride," he said.

The Man of God sermonized for a few minutes before he proceeded to his fire-brand prayer section. Indeed it was fire-brand. Tumelo wished he had postponed his attendance to another Sunday. A Sunday for another activity, other than the fire-brand prayer service of Pastor Kat. It was when the congregation rose for prayers that he saw Bontle. For the rest of the service that day, Tumelo did not concentrate on anything but Bontle, and it displeased Dineo, who kept monitoring him throughout the service.

The service ended, and Tumelo wanted to walk up to Bontle and say something to her, but he could not. She was with her parents in the Pastor's office, where the Pastor prayed for the nuclear family. They soon came out, greeted some people, and left.

Tumelo was crestfallen, and he felt like running after Mr Rufus' car when he drove off and just screaming to them that they should allow him to speak to Bontle. He really felt like doing that, but he didn't have the courage to do it.

"Tumelo, what exactly is wrong with you? You did not concentrate on anything in church, all because of a girl," Dineo said as he walked toward his friend.

"Sorry about that; I just wanted to talk to her; how can you help me? Please help me," Tumelo pleaded.

"Help you out? I cannot put my hand into anything that concerns Bontle; she's......."

"Don't start calling her names again," Tumelo interrupted. "That is quite unrighteous, don't you think so?"

'Dineo would always want to live like a saint,' thought Tumelo, 'but he could quickly dislike someone even though, as a Christian, he ought to love his neighbour.' This thinking pre-occupied Tumelo.

"It's not that I hate her or anything like that," Dineo stammered. "The problem is that Bontle is very snobbish; I see it as arrogance. Moreover, she doesn't even mingle with her peers. I think she's full of herself, and I don't like people like that. Is it because her dad is rich? Trust me. You won't like her when you get to know her better."

"I don't agree with you, and this girl cannot be that bad," Tumelo insisted.

As they walked home, he remembered the first day he saw her walking toward them in the church compound. He reminisced about how pretty she appeared. Bontle was tall and slender, with large eyes and smooth skin. Her hair fell in tangled plaits across her shoulders. She was like a freshly blossoming flower. This picture of the natural beauty she possessed remained in Tumelo's mind until he reached home that day.

"I'm happy you went to church today," his mother said after Tumelo greeted her. "I knew you to be a consistent churchgoer when we were in Serowe, but I don't know why you lost that passion here in Gaborone."

Tumelo smiled. "Mom, we can discuss that later," he said as he walked into his room.

CHAPTER THIRTEEN

Dineo was dumbfounded the day he saw Tumelo and Bontle together. He was on his way to see him when he suddenly saw the two of them in deep discussion. They were discussing the Christian faith. Bontle and Tumelo had met the previous day after the church's Bible study, but Dineo did not know. They had exchanged contact, and Bontle had promised to come to visit him so that they could discuss further the subject of new birth and salvation - a subject Tumelo subtly raised to secure her interest and attention after Bible study that day.

Bontle was raised in a Christian home; Mr and Mrs Khumo had taught her the effective practices of Christianity, the biggest of which is Evangelism. She had been taught that Evangelism was a means of laying up one's treasure in heaven and that whoever wins souls is wise and will be rewarded. She considered Tumelo a possible convert and didn't waste time on it. Moreover, it was successful; Tumelo had given his life to Christ that day, and that was what Dineo heard that finally cheered him up. He then saw Bontle from a different perspective, that she wasn't a proud peacock, especially because she was godly and heaven-conscious.

This became the genesis of a youthful Christian trio in Gaborone; Tumelo, Dineo and Bontle were like the biblical three Hebrews; they courageously spread the gospel in Gaborone and popularised the Christian faith beyond the popularity it used to have from the days of Mooketsi Tau, the grandfather of Tumelo. They converted many young folks and enlightened the dark-minded indigenes of Gaborone.

Pastor Kat was overjoyed and gave the lads all the support they needed. Mr and Mrs Rufus Khumo were more than happy that their only child Bontle was on fire for God, and Lesedi was also happy with Tumelo's newly found passion.

However, all was not well. Paticularly with Baruti Tau. Baruti would instead turn Gaborone upside down and even tear the world apart rather than allowing his father's cowardice to resurface in his first child, which is how he saw the situaton. He would rather die than allow Gaborone to preposterously elevate a foreign religion again to the detriment of their inherited traditional religion. He disowned Tumelo, resigned from Mr Khumo's company and stopped Maureen and Fenyang from following Tumelo to any church gathering.

But he was alone in this battle; the whole of Gaborone, including Boipelo, his friend, had joined the church. Most of the traditionalists had converted, and his fellow drunkards had also joined the church. Baruti became frustrated in his lone antagonism. In one of his outbursts of anger against Tumelo, who confronted him one day to preach to him, he grabbed his matchet to slaughter his own son. Tumelo ran away, but Akanyang, one of the preachers who tried to hold Baruti back from harming Tumelo, became the victim. Baruti released the cutlass on Akanyang six times until Akanyang died.

Baruti Tau knew it had all come to an end but, in his self-destructiveness, he decided to still decide on the pattern of his own demise. Before anyone could arrive for arrest or prosecution, Baruti ran away.

Everyone thought Baruti must have gone somewhere to commit suicide. Gaborone had mourned him and his victim Akanyang simultaneously, but Boipelo knew the truth. He had received a text message from an unknown phone number. He found out in the message that his friend had exiled himself to a country in West Africa, and he would never appear in Botswana again. "Not after everyone in Gaborone had chosen the path of insanity," Baruti added in the text message to show that he was still unrepentantly mad at everyone. Boipelo never stopped trying to reach him through that odd number, but it was never reachable.

Friends and families mourned him while the church mourned Akanyang, who Pastor Kat had declared a Martyr that would have a great reward in Paradise.

It was a credit to the people of Gaborone and the people of the church that the Khumo family adopted all Baruti's children, enriched his wife Lesedi, and shouldered their responsibilities.

Everyone had no doubt that Baruti Tau had angrily gone inside the Kobokwe Cave , and took to take his own life, but Boipelo knew the truth and promised himself that, if Baruti tried to return to create more havoc for innocent people, because of his own weakness and selfishness, he would reveal this truth and stop his friend from any further damage to the lives of his wife and children.